DIGGING INTO HISTORY

SOLVING THE MYSTERIES OF
STONEHENGE

Leon Gray

 **Marshall Cavendish**
Benchmark
New York

Marshall Cavendish Benchmark
99 White Plains Road
Tarrytown, New York 10591
www.marshallcavendish.us

All Web sites were available and accurate when sent to press.

Library of Congress Cataloging-in-Publication Data

Gray, Leon, 1974-
Solving the mysteries of Stonehenge / by Leon Gray.
p. cm. -- (Digging into history)
Includes bibliographical references and index.
ISBN 978-0-7614-3110-7
1. Stonehenge (England)--Juvenile literature. 2. Wiltshire (England)--Antiquities--Juvenile literature. 3. Megalithic
monuments--England--Wiltshire--Juvenile literature. I. Title.
DA142.G67 2008
936.2'319--dc22
2008002070

Picture credits
The photographs in this book are used by permission and through the courtesy of:
Front cover: John Evans/Shutterstock

AKG Images: Erich Lessing 14b, Atmosphere Picture Library 14t, Ben Plewes Travel
Photography 20–21, Roger Holfert 19, Robert Estall Photo Agency 27;
Bridgeman Art Library: 7, Ashmolean Museum, University of Oxford 8, Private Collection 11b;
Corbis: Tom Bean 26, Bettmann 25, Gianni Dagli Orti 18, Robert Estall 16, Hulton-Deutsch Collection 22,
Danny Lehman 11t, Gideon Mendel 29b, Maurice Nimmo/FLPA 21t, Paul Prince/Loop Images 28, Reuters 10,
John Wilkinson/Ecoscene 24, Adam Woolfitt 6, Adam Woolfitt/Robert Harding World Imagery 17;
© DACS 2007: AKG Images; **PA Photos:** Adam Stanford/AP 15; **Photolibrary.com:** Adam Woolfitt 29t;
Shutterstock: John Evans 4–5; **Topham:** Fortean 9, HIP 23.

Editor: Megan Comerford
Publisher: Michelle Bisson

Series created by The Brown Reference Group plc.
www.brownreference.com

Designer: Dave Allen
Picture Researcher: Clare Newman
Managing Editor: Tim Cooke
Indexer: Kay Ollerenshaw

Printed in China
1 3 5 6 4 2

Contents

WHAT IS STONEHENGE?

THE GREAT STONE CIRCLE IN SOUTHWESTERN ENGLAND IS ONE OF THE WORLD'S MOST FAMOUS ANCIENT MONUMENTS—AND ONE OF THE MOST MYSTERIOUS.

Every year on the summer solstice, usually June 21, people gather to see the sunrise at Stonehenge in southwestern England. Many are druids, who practice what they say is the religion of the ancient Britons. They claim that a similar **ritual** has been held there for thousands of years. Archaeologists are not so sure. No one really knows what the purpose of the **monument** was. There are many **theories**—but no one knows if any of them are correct.

Much of **archaeology** is concerned with discovering things that are hidden— but not at Stonehenge. The stone circle is too huge to ever be lost. It stands on a

plain near Salisbury and can be seen from miles away. Experts search for clues to how Stonehenge was built, who built it, and what it was for.

THE HANGING STONES

The stones got their name from the language of the Saxons, an ancient British people. In Saxon the name *Stonehenge* means "hanging stones." It refers to the crosspieces, or **lintels**, that lie on top of the standing stones. The stones are the most famous part of Stonehenge, but they were only the final chapter in its long construction.

Archaeologists studying Stonehenge in the 1960s used modern techniques to date items such as animal bones found buried near the stones. Things that were once alive are easier to date than stone. The findings were a surprise. They showed the monument had been built in three stages over thousands of years.

AN ANCIENT DITCH

The first builders had dug a circular ditch in the chalky earth to create a large enclosure with two entrances. They piled up the chalk inside the ditch to form a circular bank. Within the bank, they dug a ring of small holes—but seem to have filled them in again right away. The holes are called Aubrey Holes for the man who discovered them. By dating deer antlers

Some of the stones at Stonehenge have been standing for over 3,000 years. That is a remarkable feat of engineering.

Celtic Connections

In the seventeenth century John Aubrey surveyed Stonehenge and mistakenly concluded that ancient **Celts** had built it. Aubrey noticed that other stone circles stood in parts of Scotland and Ireland. Celts fled to these areas after the Romans invaded Britain in the first century C.E. Aubrey believed that all the stone circles were the work of Celtic builders. For years, people used Aubrey's theory that Stonehenge was a temple for druids, Celtic religious leaders. Later archaeologists showed that the monument was begun nearly 3,000 years before the Celts arrived in Britain. Despite these findings, people still associate Stonehenge with Celtic druids.

?
DID YOU KNOW
The Celts sacrificed people as offerings to their gods. They tied their victims up and threw them into boggy swamps to drown.

BELOW: *People dressed as druids enact a summer solstice ritual at Stonehenge.*

that ancient Britons used as tools to dig the ditch, experts date this part of Stonehenge to about 3100 B.C.E.

Stonehenge I, as archaeologists call it, was used for about 500 years and then abandoned. When Stonehenge II was built in about 2100 B.C.E., it looked different. The builders set up about eighty stone pillars in the middle of the site. These bluestones—a volcanic rock—formed two circles, one inside the other. Their entrances faced the direction of sunrise on the summer solstice.

BELOW: *Although the original circular ditch is still visible at Stonehenge, many stones have been removed for building—there is no natural stone in the area.*

Construction of Stonehenge III began in about 2000 B.C.E. The bluestones were taken down. New structures were built with huge blocks of a kind of sandstone called sarsen. In the heart of the monument was a horseshoe of arches, each formed by two tall sarsen stones joined by a horizontal lintel. The horseshoe was surrounded by a ring of sarsen stones joined by lintels.

TAKING FINAL SHAPE

Over the next 500 years, builders set out the bluestones from Stonehenge II in new patterns. Eventually, the stones were put up in a horseshoe inside the sarsen

William Stukeley

The eighteenth-century archaeologist William Stukeley, inspired by John Aubrey's studies of Stonehenge, set out to make his own careful observations of the site. He first used the term *trilithon* to describe the arches of two upright sarsen stones and a horizontal lintel. Unlike Aubrey, however, Stukeley also excavated burial mounds at and near Stonehenge. He found cremated human remains and Celtic ornaments. To Stukeley, the meaning of the findings was clear. He thought they confirmed Aubrey's theory that the monument had been used by Celtic priests known as druids. In fact, Stukeley was so convinced by the theory that he became a druid himself.

RIGHT: *Although Stukeley was wrong to connect Stonehenge with the druids, his surveys of the site were so accurate that they are still useful today.*

horseshoe, and in a circle between the sarsen horseshoe and the sarsen circle. The tallest bluestone was used to mark the line that faced the summer solstice. It is known as the Altar Stone, but was probably never used as an altar.

CLUES FROM RUINS

Today, much of Stonehenge is ruined. Stones have fallen down or been taken as construction material. But the ruins contain enough clues for experts to work out how the monument changed. They believe, for example, that Stonehenge II contained a wooden structure—perhaps a circular monument. Small variations in the soil reveal a pattern of holes in the ground that once held timber posts.

STANDING STONES

The last major work at Stonehenge took place in about 1100 B.C.E, when builders widened the entrance and cleared an avenue to the nearby Avon River. A sarsen stone called the Heel Stone marks the entrance today.

There are other individual stones, such as the Slaughter Stone, which is near the entrance. Despite the stone's name, archaeologists do not think it was ever used in **prehistoric** rituals. It is flat like a **sacrificial** altar—but only because it has fallen down. Two Station Stones stand on mounds called barrows. Most ancient barrows are built over tombs, but at Stonehenge the **barrows** are empty. They do not contain any bones or **artifacts** that might be clues to the purpose of the whole monument.

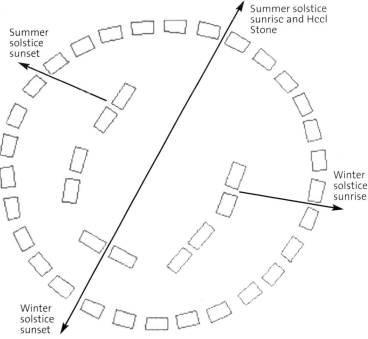

Summer solstice sunset

Summer solstice sunrise and Heel Stone

Winter solstice sunrise

Winter solstice sunset

ABOVE: *This diagram shows how the sarsen circle and trilithon horseshoe line up with the Sun on the summer and winter solstices.*

Dating Stonehenge

British archaeologist Richard Atkinson worked at Stonehenge for fourteen years. In 1956 he published a book in which he argued that the monument was built in three main stages. Today we know that he was right, although he got the exact dates wrong. Atkinson did not have access to modern dating techniques. His conclusions were based only on his detailed **excavations**.

In the 1960s, scientists used **radiocarbon dating** at the site. All living things contain carbon. After they die, the carbon steadily decays. How much carbon has decayed reveals how long ago a plant, person, or animal died. At Stonehenge, scientists dated animal and human bones buried beneath or near the stones. The results of the dating are the dates most people accept today.

TAKE A CLOSER LOOK – TAKE A CLOSER LOOK – TAKE A CLOSER LOOK – TAKE A CLOSER LOOK

Archaeology and Controversy

Stonehenge is not the only site where scientific technology has stirred up **controversy**. Around the world, other archaeological discoveries have presented evidence that clashes with people's beliefs about their ancient ancestors.

Many Scots, Irish, and Welsh, for example, celebrate their Celtic past. They believe their ancestors moved to

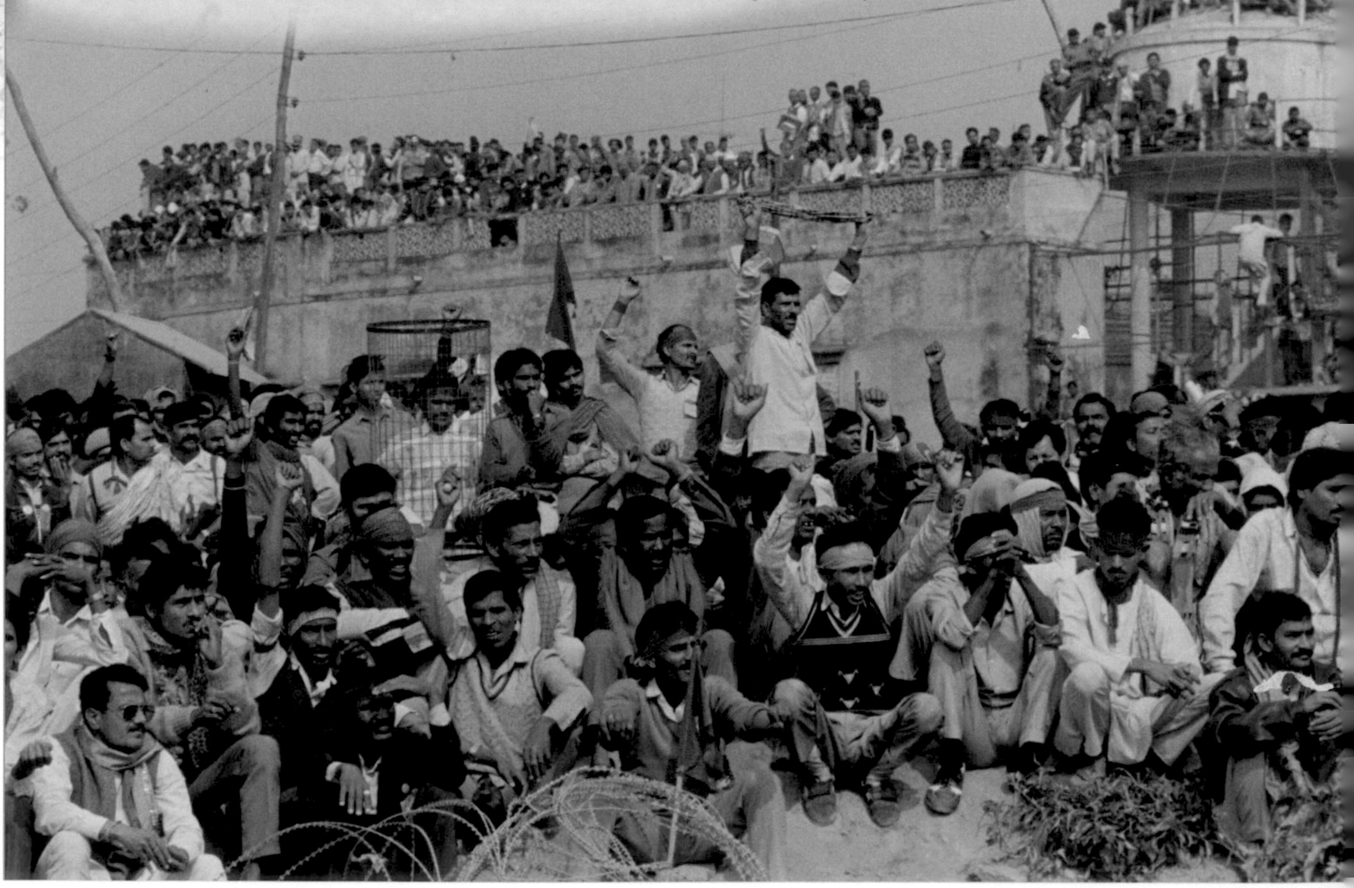

?
DID YOU KNOW

According to legend, Stonehenge is the burial spot of Boudicca, a British queen who fought the Roman occupation of Britain.

BELOW: *Hindus celebrate the destruction of a mosque at Ayodah in India in 1992. They claimed it stood on top of a Hindu temple, but surveys found no evidence of the temple.*

Britain from Europe. Modern experts using DNA testing tell a different story. DNA is a chemical that parents pass on to their children. It reveals **genetic** similarities.

The experts found that, genetically, the British have changed little over thousands of years. This may mean that although Celtic culture reached Britain, few Celts did. The people who celebrate their "Celtic" roots may be no different from other Britons. That's an argument some people do not want to hear.

In India, the Hindu and Muslim populations often clash. Hindus sometimes claim to be the original inhabitants of the land. Archaeology does not support that claim. Hindus also assert that the Muslims who arrived later built mosques on top of Hindu temples. Again, there is no evidence—but Hindus have used the argument to burn down mosques.

Another example comes from the American Southwest. Some experts claim that burned bones prove that the prehistoric

ABOVE: *The Anasazi built spectacular cliff dwellings. Their modern descendents reject the idea that people were eaten in their rituals.*

Anasazi people who lived there ate human flesh in rituals. Many modern descendents of the Anasazi do not accept that their ancestors were cannibals.

LEFT: *It is unlikely that Boudicca is buried at Stonehenge, but people still believe the myth.*

WHO BUILT STONEHENGE?

THE BUILDERS OF STONEHENGE LEFT FEW OTHER RECORDS. EXACTLY WHO THEY WERE REMAINS A MYSTERY.

All sorts of people have been put forward as the builders of Stonehenge. The ancient Romans, ancient Egyptians, and Celts have all been suggested. Dating evidence has ruled out these possibilities. Stonehenge is older than all three peoples.

There are wilder **theories**, too. Some people argued that the builders came from Atlantis, a legendary lost city, but few archaeologists believe that Atlantis existed. Another theory is that Stonehenge was built by aliens as a landing site for spacecraft.

Merlin's Magic Monument

One theory about Stonehenge was written down in the twelfth century. Geoffrey of Monmouth claimed the stones came from a monument built by giants in Ireland. When many of his soldiers died fighting the Saxons, the British king Aurelius Ambrosius wanted to erect a memorial. He had Merlin the Magician use magic to move the stones to England and rebuild them near Salisbury, where his soldiers lay buried.

FARMING PEOPLE

Although modern archaeologists use all sorts of scientific equipment, they also rely on common sense. When they ask themselves who built Stonehenge, the most obvious answer is the people who lived in the area at the time. But who were they?

The first monument at Stonehenge was built late in the Neolithic, or New Stone Age, which lasted from about 7000 B.C.E. to about 2000 B.C.E. The period marked a change in how Europeans lived. People who had moved around to hunt animals and gather fruits and berries now settled in villages. They began to grow crops and raise livestock.

Archaeologists have traced the spread of farming across Europe from West Asia. Farming brought new settlements, trading networks, technology, and beliefs—and new monuments.

LEFT: *An artist's reconstruction of how ancient peoples may have used wooden levers to move massive stones.*

SACRED PLACES

Stonehenge I was one of many **earthwork** enclosures in Britain that probably marked sacred places. The earliest enclosures were built in about 4000 B.C.E. by a people known as the Windmill Hill culture. They were some of the first farmers to settle in the Wessex region of southern England.

Sometime around 2000 B.C.E. new farmers arrived in Wessex from Europe.

They are called the Beaker folk for their bell-shaped drinking vessels. The Beaker folk were skilled at making objects from bronze and gold. They grew wealthy from trade. Beads from Wessex have been found in ancient graves as far away as Greece. Beaker tombs also contained valuable artifacts, such as weapons, so the afterlife must have been important in Beaker society.

PLACES FOR THE DEAD?

The Beaker folk built earthworks and stone circles. The wealthy rulers of Wessex may have been responsible for building the stone circles at Stonehenge. Some experts think that such structures were connected with the afterlife. Perhaps they were monuments to dead ancestors or places for rituals.

ABOVE: *The earthworks at Windmill Hill were the earliest construction of the farmers who settled in Wessex.*

ABOVE: *Archaeologists trace the spread of the Beaker folk into England by following their distinctive vessels.*

A Load of Trash

In 2006 archaeologists unearthed the remains of a large Stone Age settlement a few miles from Stonehenge at Durrington Walls. Did the builders of the monument live there? Not exactly. Excavations at the site have revealed huge amounts of Stone Age trash, such as animal bones, flints, and fragments of pottery. However, the trash suggests that the settlement was only used from time to time. Perhaps it was a site for winter solstice feasts and had some religious significance. It could also have been a stopping point for burial parties while taking the dead to Stonehenge to be **cremated** or buried.

TRASH TALKS

Piles of old trash can tell experts about:
- The food people ate
- The tools they used
- The textiles, or fabrics, they wore

BELOW: *Durrington is the largest Stone Age village ever found in Britain, but it may have been a temporary settlement.*

WHY BUILD A STONE CIRCLE?

STONEHENGE IS NOT ALONE. ACROSS EUROPE, ANCIENT BUILDERS USED HUGE STONES TO CONSTRUCT MONUMENTS THAT STILL STAND.

Circular earthworks like the one at Stonehenge are called henges. Most henges consist of a circular ditch enclosed within a bank, or a bank within a ditch, with one or more entrances. The exact purpose of henges is still not clear. They must have been important, because it took a huge effort to build them. They probably had a sacred meaning. Inside the henges, excavators have found features that might help confirm their purpose. They include pits, **postholes**, burial mounds, and standing stones.

THE GIANT STONES

Stonehenge is the most famous ancient stone monument, but it is not the only one. Neolithic peoples across Europe

erected giant stones, or **megaliths**. These monuments can consist of one or many stones.

Single stones are called menhirs. Le Grand Menhir Brisé in Brittany, the northwestern region of France, stood over 65 feet (20 meters) tall. Getting it upright was a remarkable effort. Most modern cranes would be unable to lift its 350-ton weight. The stone has since fallen down and broken into pieces.

LEFT: Castlerigg in northern England is one of the most well-preserved stone circles.

ABOVE: *Some of the houses in Avebury may have been built using stones from the monument. There is very little natural stone in the area for building.*

Avebury Rings

About 15 miles (25 kilometers) north of Stonehenge stands one of Europe's largest henges. Avebury included several rings of sarsen stones. Only a few stones still stand—most have been removed, probably for building. Their positions are marked by concrete posts to show the shape of the original monument.

Archaeology from the Air

From the air it is sometimes possible to see patterns in the landscape that are not visible from the ground. Variations in the level of the land cast shadows that cannot be seen from the ground. That makes aerial photography useful for archaeologists. In 1925 a pilot took photographs of a henge near Durrington in Wiltshire. Within the henge, circles of small depressions revealed what may have been holes for wooden posts. Over the next four years, archaeologists Edward and Maud Cunnington excavated the site. The layout of the postholes was similar to that of the bluestones at Stonehenge. It is even possible, experts guess, that the circle of posts was joined by horizontal timbers— like the sarsen stones at Stonehenge. The site is known as Woodhenge.

ABOVE: *Carnac is one of the largest arrangements of megaliths in the world.*

Menhirs are often laid out in rows or circles. Although stone circles only appear in Britain, other arrangements occur in other countries. One of the largest is at Carnac in France.

THE STONES AT CARNAC

A mile (1.6 km) north of Carnac in Brittany stand more than 3,000 stones of different shapes and sizes. Some stand alone. Most are laid out in long rows. Some stretch for half a mile and end in stone circles or fanlike arrangements.

Carnac is also home to several tumuli. A tumulus is the European equivalent of an Egyptian pyramid. High-ranking

ABOVE: *The dolmen of Lanyon Quiot, in the southern English county of Cornwall, was probably a burial chamber and may also have been used in rituals.*

people were buried in the earth mounds. Archaeologists have found that they were buried with jewelry and pottery.

Carnac also has burial chambers known as dolmens. They consist of a large horizontal stone supported by several large stones. Originally, the stones were enclosed by a mound of earth. At Carnac, however, it is mostly just the stones that remain. The earth has been removed by archaeologists or has worn away.

LEARNING TO BUILD

Experts studying megaliths in Europe have attempted to explain why they are so common. Early in the twentieth century, Australian archaeologist V. Gordon Childe noticed that most stone monuments lay along Europe's Atlantic coast. He suggested that building styles from the Mycenaean civilization of ancient Greece, which produced many megalithic monuments, were spread by travelers up the western coast of Europe. However, dating techniques in the 1960s disproved the theory. The megaliths were far older than Mycenae. Prehistoric Europeans had clearly developed their own construction technology—and their creations remain standing five millennia later.

HOW WAS STONEHENGE BUILT?

THE QUESTION OF *HOW* THE MONUMENT WAS CREATED HAS ALMOST AS MANY ANSWERS AS *WHY* IT WAS BUILT.

How did prehistoric people plan and build a structure as large as Stonehenge? They had no wheels for vehicles, animals to pull loads, compasses to check directions, or iron tools. Turning 30-ton stones upright was a huge task, but getting them to the site in the first place may have posed an even greater problem.

Geologists are scientists who are experts in rocks. They can analyze the chemicals in a rock to identify where it came from. They have discovered that

the sarsen stones at Stonehenge came from a quarry near Avebury, which is about 25 miles (40 km) away. The bluestones are smaller but may have been brought an even greater distance.

AN EXPERIMENT
In the 1950s, archaeologist Richard Atkinson suggested that workers used ropes to pull the sarsen stones across the ground on wooden sleds, perhaps using rollers, too. He got his students to test his theory. It took thirty-two people to drag a 1.5-ton block of stone only a

BELOW: *The Preseli Hills in Wales are the only natural source of the exact kind of bluestone (above) used at Stonehenge.*

Prehistoric Technology

It is remarkable that anyone could build a monument like Stonehenge without bulldozers or cranes—or even wheels. There were no hand tools such as shovels or pickaxes. There were no iron tools. But people had learned to use sharp flakes of stone, such as flint or **obsidian**, for knives and used animal bones and antlers to dig in the earth. They made ropes by weaving together plant fibers or animal sinew. They may have moved heavy loads by rolling them along on tree trunks. Tree trunks might also have been used as prehistoric lifting machines, acting as giant levers.

hundred yards—and the stones at Stonehenge weigh 20 to 30 tons.

Atkinson estimated that with 1,500 workers—a huge number at a time when most villages were small—it would have taken nine weeks to move each block to Stonehenge. To move all eighty-one sarsen stones would have taken at least five years and probably twice as long.

SHAPING THE STONES

Once the stones got to the site, there was more work to be done. Archaeologists have found round stones called mauls,

which range in size from baseballs to soccer balls. Workers used the mauls to dress, or shape, the stones and make the surface as smooth as possible.

Mauls were also used to shape joints for the lintels. Each upright stone had a cone-shaped lump on top, called a tenon. The tenons slotted into hollows called mortises on the bottom of the lintels.

RAISING THE STONES

When the stones were ready, they had to be lifted into place. Some archaeologists think that a large timber A-frame was built above a hole dug for a stone. Teams of workers then used ropes passing over the frame to pull the stone upright.

Another idea is that a stone was hauled up an earth ramp and its end tipped into a ditch. Ropes and levers could then be used to get the stone fully upright before the ramp was removed.

The huge lintels had to be raised more than 20 feet (6.2 m) to the top of the uprights. Again, they may have been hauled up earth ramps. But there is no sign that such huge quantities of earth were ever moved at the site.

LEFT: *When some fallen stones were restored to their original positions in 1964, the best way to lift them was clear—with a crane!*

LEFT: *This lintel stone now lies on the ground. It shows the hollowed-out mortises that join with the tenons on top of the upright stones.*

?

DID YOU KNOW

Mortises and tenons were first used in woodwork. The sarsens would probably have stood up without them, because of their great weight.

Another theory is that lintels were raised on a criss-cross frame of layers of logs. Levers raised each end of the lintel a few inches so a new log was inserted beneath the stone. By repeating this process many times at each end of the stone, workers gradually raised it to the right height before sliding it into position.

Some or all of these techniques may have helped build Stonehenge, but we may never know for sure.

A Bluestone Mystery

Geologists have matched the bluestones at Stonehenge to rocks from the Preseli Hills of South Wales, 135 miles (215 km) away. Experts once believed that the ancient builders moved the bluestones the whole way by boat around the coast and along rivers. Today, some archaeologists think this is only part of the story. Huge blocks of ice called glaciers moved across South Wales during the last ice age, when the temperatures all over Earth grew colder. The glaciers may have picked up bluestones from Wales and carried them to southern England. Experts think the glaciers deposited the stones near Stonehenge, so they were easy for the builders to collect.

Experimental Archaeology

Modern archaeologists and engineers have made a number of attempts to test how Stonehenge was built. In the 1950s, Richard Atkinson used a team of students to haul a rock over land on a wooden sled constructed using materials that would have been available to prehistoric builders. They also floated a large rock on three flat-bottomed boats to show how the bluestones may have been transported from Wales.

A later attempt to move a stone over the route from the Preseli Hills started well. Volunteers dragged the stone on a sled from the

BELOW: *At this reconstructed Iron Age village in England, experts try to grow crops that ancient farmers grew using the same farming techniques.*

LEFT: *The raft* Ra II *sets sail across the Atlantic in 1970. Its crew built it from reeds based on ancient drawings to prove that the ancient Egyptians traveled to Mexico by sea. The* Ra II *completed the journey in 57 days, but that only showed that ancient people could have made the journey—not that they did.*

hills to the sea. But when it was placed on a specially built raft, the raft sank. In the mid-1990s a British team used wooden A-frames and ropes like those available in the Stone Age to build a massive concrete trilithon. The experiment was a success, but it did not prove that Stonehenge was built in the same way.

TRIAL AND ERROR

Attempts to reconstruct the past are known as experimental archaeology. Archaeologists try to perform a task using the same materials or tools people used in the past. With expertise and common sense, archaeologists try to figure out how ancient people might have done something, from building a boat to baking bread to melting iron for tool production.

Sometimes the process involves a lot of trial and error. Experts who tried to make cement like the ancient Romans found that the first wall they built fell down when it rained. The team continued trying until they got the mixture right.

Some archaeologists re-create entire ancient villages. Volunteers have tried living in Iron Age villages in Denmark and Britain, for example. The experience can reveal a lot about the past—but it can be risky. In one experiment everyone got sick because of the poor diet!

WHAT DO WE KNOW?

AFTER CENTURIES OF INVESTIGATION, WE ARE ONLY A LITTLE CLOSER TO UNDERSTANDING THE TRUE MEANING OF STONEHENGE.

British archaeologist Richard Atkinson probably knew more about Stonehenge than anyone else. He got impatient when people tried to guess what it was for. He said, "Most of what has been written about Stonehenge is nonsense or speculation. No one will ever have a clue what its significance was."

That has not stopped people from trying to guess. Archaeologists—and many amateurs—are still trying to unlock the mysteries of Stonehenge. It may have served several different purposes over time.

CEREMONIAL SITE

Many people now think that Stonehenge was built as a ceremonial site for the dead. Burial sites are dotted around the site. Some of the Aubrey Holes are filled with ashes from burned human remains. According to one theory, Stonehenge marked the end of a **funeral** journey. Mourners passed sacred sites along the Avon River to reach Stonehenge at sunset. There is no proof of this theory, however. It has been deduced from the location of the sites—but that may be a coincidence. We do not even know if the sites were all connected in the minds of the people who built them.

LEFT: *Stonehenge is one of the most recognizable of all ancient sites—and one of the most imitated. This "carhenge" is in Nebraska.*

Some evidence is clear. The builders of Stonehenge were skilled architects and **astronomers**. The standing stones are laid out to mark where the sun rises and sets on the summer solstice and the winter solstice—the longest and shortest

ABOVE: *Expert Richard Atkinson was amazed to find faint carvings, or petroglyphs, that represented ancient weapons on a sarsen stone.*

A False Start

In 1953 Richard Atkinson was photographing the sarsen stones in the inner horseshoe when he noticed faint carvings that resembled a dagger and prehistoric axes (above). The dagger matched daggers from Mycenae in ancient Greece. Some experts took this as proof that Stonehenge was the work of the Mycenaeans. In fact, it only provided a reliable date for the carving since the weapons appeared in Mycenae after 1470 B.C.E.

27

Stonehenge Decoded

In 1963 U.S. astronomer Gerald Hawkins plotted the positions of the standing stones and other features of Stonehenge on an early computer. He used the computer to model the movements of the Sun and Moon. Hawkins identified 165 key alignments of lines from the Sun and the Moon through the station stones and the Heel Stone. He published a book, *Stonehenge Decoded*, suggesting that Stonehenge was an ancient computer that predicted solar and lunar eclipses. The theory was dismissed by most experts—but the book became a bestseller.

ANCIENT COMPUTERS

Some experts suggest these ancient sites were also used to track heavenly bodies:
- Machu Picchu, Peru
- Angkor, Cambodia
- Chaco Canyon, U.S.
- Sphinx, Egypt
- Pyramids, Egypt

BELOW: *Was Stonehenge a tool for following the movement of the Sun in the sky?*

days of the year. On the summer solstice, the Sun rises directly above the Heel Stone. On the winter solstice, it sets directly opposite it.

FARMERS' CALENDAR

Some archaeologists think later versions of Stonehenge helped farmers to chart the changing seasons and judge when to plant their crops. Again, there is no proof. But prehistoric farmers around the world did build monuments with similar astronomical alignments.

Among those who believe Stonehenge has an astronomical meaning arc the

ABOVE: *The Heel Stone (right) marks the line of the sunrise on the summer and winter solstices.*

people who gather there for every summer solstice. Perhaps they really are following in the footsteps of their ancient ancestors.

BELOW: *Summer solstice celebrations at Stonehenge are still popular today—and not just with druids!*

Further Resources

BOOKS

Chippindale, Christopher. *Stonehenge Complete* (third edition). New York: Thames and Hudson, 2004.

Doeden, Matt. *Stonehenge*. Mankato, MN: Capstone Press, 2007.

Lace, William. *Stonehenge* (The Mystery Library). San Diego, CA: Lucent Books, 2003.

WEB SITES

BBC Wiltshire site with a 360° gallery from inside the circle
http://www.bbc.co.uk/wiltshire/moonraking/landscape_stonehenge.shtml

The official Stonehenge site from English Heritage
http://www.english-heritage.org.uk/server/show/nav.876

PBS case file on Murder at Stonehenge
http://www.pbs.org/wnet/secrets/case_stonehenge/index.html

The Stone Pages guide to megaliths in Europe
http://www.stonepages.com/

Glossary

archaeology: The scientific study of cultures by analyzing remains such as artifacts and monuments.

artifact: An object that has been made or changed by humans.

astronomy: The scientific study of the movement of heavenly bodies.

barrow: A mound of earth over a tomb.

Celt: A member of a group of peoples who lived in central Europe from about 800 B.C.E until about 500 C.E.

controversy: A dispute between people with widely different views.

cremate: To burn a dead body to dispose of it.

earthwork: A structure made by shaping the ground.

excavation: A scientific dig to explore an archacological site.

funeral: The religious ceremony held to dispose of a dead body.

genetic: Relating to genes, which pass qualities from parents to their children.

lintel: A horizontal stone or timber above an opening or doorway,

megalith: A large stone used in monuments.

monument: A structure meant as a lasting celebration of a person, event, or other subject.

obsidian: A hard, glasslike rock used in the ancient world to make blades for tools and weapons.

posthole: A pit dug in the ground to support a wooden or stone pillar.

prehistoric: Before recorded history.

radiocarbon dating: A way to find the age of something that was once alive by analyzing how much of its carbon has decayed.

ritual: A ceremony carried out as part of religious worship.

sacrifice: An offering to the gods, sometimes involving the killing of an animal or a person.

theory: The explanation that best fits the available facts.

Names to Know

Atkinson, Richard (1920–1994). British archaeologist who directed excavations at Stonehenge between 1950 and 1964.

Aubrey, John (1626–1697). English writer who surveyed ancient sites in Wiltshire, including Stonehenge.

Childe, V. Gordon (1892–1957). Australian archaeologist who specialized in prehistoric peoples.

Cunnington, Edward and Maud. Husband and wife team who excavated the first woodhenge in the 1920s.

Stukeley, William (1687–1765). A pioneer of archaeology and one of the first to work at Stonehenge and examine ancient remains in the field.

Index